ARE YOU GOING THROUGH A CRISIS?

ALSO FROM REVIVAL TODAY

Financial Overflow

Dominion Over Sickness and Disease

Boldly I Come

Twenty Secrets for an Unbreakable Marriage

How to Dominate in a Wicked Nation

Seven Wrong Relationships

Everything a Man Should Be

Understanding the World in Light of Bible Prophecy

Are You Going Through a Crisis?

Books are available in EBOOK and PAPERBACK through your favorite online book retailer or by request from your local bookstore.

ARE YOU GOING THROUGH A CRISIS?

10 KEYS TO EMERGE AS A CHAMPION

JONATHAN SHUTTLESWORTH

Unless otherwise indicated, all Scripture quotations are taken from the Holy Bible, New Living Translation, copyright © 1996, 2004, 2015 by Tyndale House Foundation. Used by permission of Tyndale House Publishers, a Division of Tyndale House Ministries, Carol Stream, Illinois 60188. All rights reserved.

Book design by eBook Prep: www.ebookprep.com

April 2023

ISBN: 978-1-64457-296-2

Rise UP Publications
644 Shrewsbury Commons Ave, Ste 249
Shrewsbury PA 17361
United States of America
www.riseUPpublications.com
Phone: 866-846-5123

CONTENTS

If you maintain your joy, you maintain your strength.

— JONATHAN SHUTTLESWORTH

INTRODUCTION

The Bible is not something to disengage from when you're going through a hard time and then come back to when you have your problem solved. Neither is the Bible written to help successful people become slightly more successful. God told Samuel in the Old Testament, *"I take the beggar from the dunghill and set him among princes."*

The Bible actually gives you a roadmap out of a crisis. The Bible provides the power to get through a crisis.

> The thief cometh not, but for to steal, and to
> kill, and to destroy: I am come that they
> might have life, and that they might
> have it more abundantly.

— JOHN 10:10 (KJV)

Jesus didn't come so you could just survive and endure life. He came so you could enjoy life. *"I have come that you might have life, and have it more abundantly."* Jesus didn't come so you could hold on until you die. He came so you can enjoy life.

I want to deal with the "Devil" part of the verse: *"The thief comes to steal, and to kill."* Now you might think, how can you further harm someone after killing them? Because it doesn't just say, "steal and kill," it says "steal, kill and *destroy.*"

One crisis people face is death. Death is an enemy—death is a harsh enemy. If you've had somebody die an early death—a husband, a wife, a parent, a child—I want you to understand that the Devil has a will. It wasn't God's will for that person to die early; that's an attack of the enemy. The Devil comes to destroy and to kill.

Suppose you're reading this and your wife recently died in a car accident. Well, she's gone. Now, you have to focus on controlling the things you can control. If the Devil has his way, he won't stop with your wife; he'll use your wife's death to destroy your faith, destroy your health and assure you're medicated for the rest of your life. You won't be able to work or even leave the house. You'll be tormented by thoughts of what happened or what you should have done to prevent it.

If you're in a situation like this, you have to focus on not letting this loss destroy your mind, family, and household. Whatever you've lost to this point, you must put a stop to any further losses.

KEY #1

VICTORY BELONGS TO YOU

Those who trust in the Lord are as secure as
Mount Zion; they will not be defeated
but will endure forever.

— PSALM 125:1

Whether you feel like it or not, you are more than a conqueror. You certainly don't feel like a conqueror when you're going through a difficult time. But you are what the Bible says you are; you're not a victim or an easily defeated person. The Bible says, *"they will not be defeated."* So you have a scriptural right to be victorious; it's not that you're trying to get something that doesn't belong to you. There's an old saying: "It's difficult to hit a small target, but it's impossible to hit a target you don't have."

The Devil will try to convince you that victory is impossible; you've been attacked, the situation is irreparable, you'll always be a victim, and you'll struggle with this every day—by no coincidence, this is also what secular counseling will teach you as well.

This is what the Bible says, *"Those who trust in the Lord are as secure as Mount Zion; they will not be defeated but will endure forever."*

KEY #2

DO NOT ISOLATE YOURSELF

Then he went on alone into the wilderness, traveling all day. He sat down under a solitary broom tree and prayed that he might die. "I have had enough, LORD," he said. "Take my life, for I am no better than my ancestors who have already died." Then he lay down and slept under the broom tree. But as he was sleeping, an angel touched him and told him, "Get up and eat!" He looked around and there beside his head was some bread baked on hot stones and a jar of water! So he ate and drank and lay down again.

— 1 KINGS 19: 4-6

Elijah had just won a great victory in this verse, having called fire down from heaven. He sat underneath a broom tree and prayed that he might die, and an angel came and encouraged him.

When you're going through a difficult time, your soul and your flesh want to shut yourself in a room, turn the lights off, and crawl under the covers—you want to disengage.

A man's wife passes away, and no one has seen him in three weeks. He stays away from church. Remember, one of the first things God said was, "It's not good for a man to be alone." One thing Satan aimed to do during the Coronavirus pandemic was to isolate many people—no in-person church, "stay home and save lives." As a result, occurrences of depression, alcoholism, drug overdose, and suicide went through the roof.

Fight the urge. When you're going through a difficult time, you don't want to talk to anybody. You don't want to hear people saying stupid things to you. If you lost a child, you know someone will come up to you and say something dumb. Some "prophetic person" will come up and say something ridiculous, trying to be spiritual.

But this is really important: When somebody comes up to you and says something stupid, regardless of what their words are, just hear, "I love you," because that's all they're really trying to say. They're hurting too; they don't know what to say. Ignore the words; just realize they're trying to say, "I love you." They feel bad for you. They're trying to say something to encourage you, but they're not at their best.

Resist the urge to isolate. If the Devil gets you by yourself, it's easier to discourage and destroy you. That's where Elijah found himself in 1 Kings 19. It's interesting that right after that, God hooked him up with a good buddy, Elisha.

KEY #3

FAST AND PRAY

And when he came to his disciples, he saw
a great multitude about them, and the
scribes questioning with them. And
straightway all the people, when they
beheld him, were greatly amazed, and
running to him saluted him. And he
asked the scribes, What question ye
with them? And one of the multitude
answered and said, Master, I have
brought unto thee my son, which hath a
dumb spirit; And wheresoever he taketh
him, he teareth him: and he foameth,
and gnasheth with his teeth, and pineth
away: and I spake to thy disciples that
they should cast him out; and they could
not. He answereth him, and saith, O
faithless generation, how long shall I be
with you? how long shall I suffer you?
bring him unto me. And they brought

him unto him: and when he saw him, straightway the spirit tare him; and he fell on the ground, and wallowed foaming. And he asked his father, How long is it ago since this came unto him? And he said, Of a child. And ofttimes it hath cast him into the fire, and into the waters, to destroy him: but if thou canst do any thing, have compassion on us, and help us. Jesus said unto him, If thou canst believe, all things are possible to him that believeth. And straightway the father of the child cried out, and said with tears, Lord, I believe; help thou mine unbelief. When Jesus saw that the people came running together, he rebuked the foul spirit, saying unto him, Thou dumb and deaf spirit, I charge thee, come out of him, and enter no more into him. And the spirit cried, and rent him sore, and came out of him: and he was as one dead; insomuch that many said, He is dead. But Jesus took him by the hand, and lifted him up; and he arose. And when he was come into the house, his disciples asked him privately, Why could not we cast him out? And he said unto them, This kind can come forth by nothing, but by prayer and fasting.

— MARK 9:14-29 (KJV)

F asting is effective. I don't mean 100 days. I don't mean 40 days. I don't even mean 21 days like we do at the beginning of every year to commit that year to God. But for something like this, you don't have to go for more than three days. I would fast for three days and pray because fasting without praying is just a hunger strike.

Why fast and pray? Because fasting and prayer is a platform for breakthrough. Fasting and prayer doesn't only change you, fasting and prayer changes *things*. Fasting and prayer, in Mark 9, were noted by Jesus as necessary for healing a deaf and mute boy who suffered from seizures, and the seizures stopped.

When COVID hit in March 2020, gatherings were restricted to 10 or less and then expanded to no public gatherings. Everything seemed to point to our ministry as having the worst year we've ever had. I went on a fast. Plus, Pastor Rodney had just gotten arrested. I'm not going to sit home and eat while he's in prison. So, I fasted. Even after he was released, I just stayed on the fast, because I thought whatever's going to happen this year, and whatever I'm up against, I want to know that I gave it my all spiritually. That's what fasting and prayer does. You need to fast and pray and shut yourself in with God for some time. Remember, not more than three days.

It's often easy to fast when a crisis hits because you don't feel like eating anyway. If you get a phone call that somebody embezzled $2.5 million from your business, that doesn't make you hungry. It feels like a punch in the stomach. You already don't feel like eating. You just go on a fast and pray when you get news like that. I'm not saying you have to go through a crisis to fast, but this book is for people going through crises.

Fast and pray. Take three days and pour out your heart to God.

KEY #4

DON'T LOSE YOUR JOY

"Go and enjoy choice food and sweet
drinks, and send some to those who
have nothing prepared. This day is holy
to our Lord. Do not grieve, for the joy
of the Lord is your strength."

— NEHEMIAH 8:10 (NIV)

D on't lose your joy. Why? The joy of the Lord is
your strength.

The vine dries up; the fig tree languishes.
Pomegranate, palm, and apple, all the
trees of the field are dried up,
and gladness dries up from the children
of man.

— JOEL 1:12 (ESV)

> With joy you will draw water from the
> wells of salvation.
>
> — ISAIAH 12:3 (ESV)

Everything you've been given in redemption is accessed by joy.

Here's a strange scripture…

> The vine is dried up, and the fig tree
> languisheth; the pomegranate tree, the
> palm tree also, and the apple
> tree, even all the trees of the field, are
> withered: because joy is withered away
> from the sons of men.
>
> — JOEL 1:12

It's not natural, when you lose someone or get news that somebody embezzled money from your business, to say, "Well, you got to keep your joy." But you have to, by your spirit and by the Holy Spirit, learn to laugh at the Devil. You must laugh at defeat and say, "You might have taken this, but you're not going to take my joy." If you concede your joy, you're going to lose the battle. If you maintain your joy, you maintain your strength.

Praying out of sorrow and defeat won't get you anywhere. Saying, "Heavenly Father," then whining for 30 minutes, and then saying, "In Jesus name, we pray, Amen," is not prayer. That's not the kind of prayer that effects anything. You have to stir up your faith. People will pray and fast, but the only prayer that helps anything is the prayer of faith.

When David was in major trouble and people were talking about killing him, David encouraged himself in the Lord by putting on the garment of praise for the spirit of heaviness. Not the garment of worship, but the garment of *praise*. When you feel discouraged, even if you're going to put on Christian music, you feel like putting on slow Christian music. You need high-praise music; there's not a lot that exists anymore. Look up G.E. Patterson's old music, or Israel Houghton's old stuff. Good praise music has an anointing on it that destroys heaviness. Secular music has great stuff to soothe your soul, but it'll keep you defeated.

Put on the garment of praise for the spirit of heaviness.

Never allow the Devil to take your joy. If the Devil gets you to forfeit your joy, he has you beat, no matter how much you pray and fast. The joy of the Lord is your strength.

KEY #5

TALK ABOUT IT WITH GOD AND PEOPLE
WHO CAN DIRECTLY HELP YOU
—THAT'S ALL

You may want to talk about your problem with everybody, but later you'll wish you hadn't. Tell God. Tell people who can directly help you, and that's all. Because the storm will pass, and you'll regret crying to someone who doesn't necessarily care and couldn't help anyway. You never feel good by talking about bad things. So, if you take time and tell everybody what you're going through, you're not going to feel better afterward. It may feel good while you're doing it because you're unburdening your soul, but ultimately, you never feel good by talking about bad things.

KEY #6

YOUR ENEMY ALWAYS MAKES MISTAKES

Throughout the Bible, people who planned against God's children usually slipped up. It's true today. Files get deleted. Paperwork gets misfiled. My friend, who was facing 90 days in jail for keeping his church open and not forcing his congregation to be vaccinated, won his case. The judge didn't show up on his court date, so they got another judge, and that judge liked him.

Don't allow the Devil to get you thinking your enemy is invulnerable. That's why nobody took Goliath on. You're not fighting against God. Even if you're fighting against the Devil himself, he makes a lot of mistakes. The Devil's greatest plan was to crucify Jesus. How did that work out for him?

Your enemy will always make a mistake. Haman had a full-proof plan to kill all the Jews, and he messed up. He hung on his own gallows.

KEY #7

YOUR ENEMY HAS NO POWER OVER YOU

My enemy is not in dominion over me; I have dominion over my enemy.

> Herein is our love made perfect, that we
>   may have boldness in the day of
>   judgment: because as he is, so are we in
>   this world.
>
> — 1 JOHN 4:17 (KJV)

As Jesus is now, so are we in this world.

Did Pilate have authority over Jesus in the natural? Yes, he did. But what did Jesus say to him? "You have no power over me whatsoever, except what's been given to you by my father. No man takes my life from me. I lay it down willingly." Every time they tried to kill Jesus before it was his time, nobody could lay a hand on Him. One time He disappeared. Another time, He walked through them, and nobody dared lay a hand on Him.

If Jesus tells me to start a church and somebody with authority (on paper) tries to stop me, do they have authority over me? Yes. Do they actually have the ability to exercise power over me? No, they don't. I will build my church, and the gates of hell will not prevail against it.

Regardless of their authority on paper, your enemy has no power over you. The Devil is not over your head; the Devil is under your feet. If the Devil himself is under your feet, how much further under your feet are the people who work for him or represent him?

KEY #8

YOU'RE INTELLIGENT AND ABLE TO OUTTHINK YOUR ENEMY

For who hath known the mind of the Lord,
that he may instruct him? but we have
the mind of Christ.

— 1 CORINTHIANS 2:16 (KJV)

It irritates me when I hear people talk about how depressed they are. That's not how your mind is supposed to work.

Write this down, and confess it regularly: *"I have the mind of Christ."*

What does that mean in reference to dealing with a crisis? You are more intelligent than your enemy, and you can outthink your enemy. They might be making a plan against you, but with your God-anointed mind, you can outthink them and launch a counter-strategy. Make a plan to beat them. Make a plan to win. Don't sit back and hope things go away. Make a plan. Outthink your enemy.

33

I refuse to be one of those Christians worried about what the Illuminati or the World Economic Forum is planning. They don't have what we have. You have a mind—you have Christ's mind.

What was Christ's mind like in practical operation? They sent the smartest people, the smartest legal experts, to trap Jesus Christ, and He answered them in a way that shamed them. He didn't give them a good answer. He made them look stupid. The smartest people they sent to make Him look stupid, He spoke something that made them look stupid. He shamed his enemies with His superior mind, which is yours in Christ. *We have the mind of Christ* (1 Corinthians 2:16).

You can outthink your enemy. They're not smarter than you. You can win. Outthink them. Use that mind. Make a plan. You see this throughout the Bible. God gave His children a strategy. It didn't matter what it was. It might have been something that makes no sense in the natural—march around Jericho, then give a shout and watch the walls fall flat. He gave David the idea for smooth stones instead of traditional weapons such as a sword and shield.

KEY #9

STRENGTHEN YOUR FAITH

I 've had several people ask me: How do I not doubt? How do I avoid unbelief when I'm going through a difficult time?

Faith and fear can't reside in the same place. Faith and unbelief can't reside in the same place, either. Likewise, faith and sorrow can't really reside in the same place. Instead of trying to get rid of doubt, if you prefill the vessel with faith, there's no room for fear or unbelief, or sorrow. The key is to fill yourself with faith. But how do you get faith? You can't sing for faith. You can't pray for faith. Faith essentially comes one way...

> Faith cometh by hearing, and hearing by the
> word of God.

> — ROMANS 10:17 (KJV)

Faith cometh by hearing the Word of God preached, and the Word of God taught.

Your mind can only wonder and think about negative things if you leave it open. I didn't make the Revival Today app for the fun of it; I did it to give people a source for faith-filled preaching and teaching.

> I remember your genuine faith, for you share the faith that first filled your grandmother Lois and your mother, Eunice. And I know that same faith continues strong in you. This is why I remind you to fan into flames the spiritual gift God gave you when I laid my hands on you. For God has not given us a spirit of fear and timidity, but of power, love, and self-discipline.
>
> — 2 TIMOTHY 1:5-7

What's timidity? "I just don't know how things are going to work out. They said that they're not going to allow us." —that's timidity.

God has not given us a spirit of fear and humility. What did He give you instead? Love, power, and soundness of mind. And that comes from the Word. Listen to the Word of God preached.

KEY #10

REFUSE TO WORRY

Do not be anxious or worried about
   anything, but in everything [every
   circumstance and situation] by prayer
   and petition with thanksgiving, continue
   to make your [specific] requests known
   to God. And the peace of God [that
   peace which reassures the heart, that
   peace] which transcends all
   understanding, [that peace which]
   stands guard over your hearts and your
   minds in Christ Jesus [is yours].

— PHILIPPIANS 4:6-7 (AMP)

Commit your concerns to God in prayer and refuse to entertain them in your mind after that. The next time the Devil tries to get you to worry about that thing, say right out loud, "I already gave that problem to God."

Cast all your cares and anxieties on Him for He cares for you. Don't cast it on Him and then take it back.

"I've given that to God. I'm not thinking about it anymore. I'm not entertaining it in my thought life anymore. I'm done. I gave that to God. I've entrusted it to Him. I'm done. You're not getting me to think about it. I'm not bringing it up."

When you hear people bringing up the same things all the time, you know they haven't prayed, because if they'd prayed correctly, they'd be confident.

"I've given that to God. He's heard me. He's answered me. It's done. I don't call it done when I see the result. I call it done when I'm finished praying."

My father prayed that way. When I was growing up, he'd close prayer by saying, "We received it and call it done in Jesus' name. Amen." You should finish your prayers like that. "We received it. I receive it now. I call it done. I'm done."

Faith calls it done, and I'm not worrying about it. The Bible tells me not to worry. I've given it to the Lord. I can trust in Him. He's too faithful to fail. I'm not worrying about an enemy that I'm smarter and stronger than.

Speak these things:

- "I'm too strong for my enemy."
- "In Christ, I'm too strong for depression."
- "I'm too strong for suicidal thoughts."
- "I'm too strong to be taken out by my enemy."
- "If God is for me, who can be against me?"

- "There's more with us than there are with them."
- "I'm too strong for my enemies." That's what you should say out loud when the enemy tries to get you to worry about the thing again.
- "Thank you, Jesus, that I'm too strong by redemption. I'm too strong for my enemies. The same way the enemy couldn't keep you in that tomb, he can't keep me where he wants to put me because I live by your resurrection life."

God never said you wouldn't have any enemies. He said, "When your enemy attacks you from one direction, I will make them run from you in seven directions." Laugh in the face of the Devil.

Speak it: "Victory belongs to me because I belong to Jesus."

Jesus already had the victory. He didn't come to the earth to get victory for himself. He came to Earth to get victory for you and me.

AFTERWORD

The Bible is what you should cling to when you're facing a crisis, not just when life is easy. The Bible provides you with the power necessary to get through a crisis with victory. Jesus didn't come so you could just endure life and hold on until you die; Jesus came so you can enjoy life. If you're in the middle of a crisis, you can't let it destroy your mind, family, and household. Here are the 10 keys to facing a crisis like a champion, as we discussed in this book.

1. Victory belongs to you. Although you may not feel like it while you're going through a tough time, the Bible says those who trust in the Lord will endure forever.
2. Do not isolate yourself. When going through a crisis, your "flesh" wants to shut you in a dark room alone. Resist the urge. If the Devil gets you by yourself, it's easier to discourage you.

3. Fast and pray. This is a platform for breakthrough. Prayer and fasting doesn't just change you, it changes things. Take three days to fast and pray to pour your heart out to God when a crisis comes.

4. Don't lose your joy. The joy of the Lord is your strength; everything you've been given in redemption is accessed by joy.

5. Only talk about your crisis with God and with people who can directly help you. You never feel good when talking about bad things; while it may feel good to rant about your problems in the moment, you'll always regret it.

6. Your enemy always makes mistakes. People who plan against God's children always slip up—files get deleted, paperwork gets misfiled, plans fall through. Just like Haman, your enemy will hang on their own gallows.

7. Your enemy has no power over you. Regardless of their authority on paper, your enemy has no power over you. The Devil is under your feet.

8. You're intelligent and able to outthink your enemy. You have the mind of Christ, and you can use that mind to outthink your enemy. God gives His children strategy.

9. Strengthen your faith. Faith and fear cannot reside in the same place. The key is to prefill your vessel with faith; faith comes by hearing the Word of God.

10. Refuse to worry. After you've prayed, faith calls it done; the Bible tells you not to worry about it. If you've given it to the Lord, you can trust Him. He is too faithful to fail.

"My generation shall be saved!"

— JONATHAN
SHUTTLESWORTH

ABOUT THE AUTHOR

Evangelist and Pastor, Jonathan Shuttlesworth, is the founder of Revival Today and Pastor of Revival Today Church, ministries dedicated to reaching lost and hurting people with The Gospel of Jesus Christ.

In fulfilling his calling, Jonathan Shuttlesworth has conducted meetings and open-air crusades throughout North America, India, the Caribbean, and Central and South Africa.

Revival Today Church was launched in 2022 as a soul-winning, Holy Spirit honoring church that is unapologetic about believing the Bible to bless families and nations.

Each day thousands of lives are impacted globally through Revival Today Broadcasting and Revival Today Church, located in Pittsburgh, Pennsylvania.

While methods may change, Revival Today's heartbeat remains for the lost, providing biblical teaching on faith, healing, prosperity, freedom from sin, and living a victorious life.

If you need help or would like to partner with Revival Today to see this generation and nation transformed through The Gospel, follow these links…

CONTACT REVIVAL TODAY

www.RevivalToday.com
www.RevivalTodayChurch.com

Get access to our 24/7 network Revival Today Global Broadcast. Download the Revival Today app in your Apple App Store or Google Play Store. Watch live on Apple TV, Roku, Amazon Fire TV, and Android TV.

facebook.com/revivaltoday

twitter.com/jdshuttlesworth

instagram.com/jdshuttlesworth

youtube.com/@jonathanshuttlesworth